W9-BZX-305

Building Character

Being Grateful

by Rebecca Pettiford

Bullfrog Books

Ideas for Parents and Teachers

Bullfrog Books let children practice reading informational text at the earliest reading levels. Repetition, familiar words, and photo labels support early readers.

Before Reading

- Discuss the cover photo. What does it tell them?

- Look at the picture glossary together. Read and discuss the words.

Read the Book

- "Walk" through the book and look at the photos. Let the child ask questions. Point out the photo labels.

- Read the book to the child, or have him or her read independently.

After Reading

- Prompt the child to think more. Ask: What are you grateful for? How do you show your gratitude?

Bullfrog Books are published by Jump!
5357 Penn Avenue South
Minneapolis, MN 55419
www.jumplibrary.com

Library of Congress Cataloging-in-Publication Data

Names: Pettiford, Rebecca, author.
Title: Being grateful / by Rebecca Pettiford.
Description: Minneapolis, MN: Jump!, Inc., [2017]
Series: Building character | Audience: K to Grade 3.
Includes index.
Identifiers: LCCN 2017023776 (print)
LCCN 2017021157 (ebook)
ISBN 9781624966422 (ebook)
ISBN 9781620318768 (hardcover: alk. paper)
ISBN 9781620318775 (pbk.)
Subjects: LCSH: Gratitude—Juvenile literature.
Classification: LCC BF575.G68 (print)
LCC BF575.G68 P48 2017 (ebook) | DDC 179/.9—dc23
LC record available at https://lccn.loc.gov/2017023776

Editor: Kirsten Chang
Book Designer: Michelle Sonnek
Photo Researcher: Michelle Sonnek

Photo Credits: Photoevent/iStock, cover, 3; Rawpixel.com/Shutterstock, cover; Nicole S. Young/iStock, 1; SusaZoom/Shutterstock, 4, 23tl; Sergey Novikov/Shutterstock, 5, 14; Tiger Images/Shutterstock, 6; James Davies/Alamy, 6–7; jonya/iStock, 8; Rob Marmion/Shutterstock, 9; wavebreakmedia/Shutterstock, 10–11, 12–13, 20–21, 23br; michaeljung/Shutterstock, 15, 23tr; Tomasz Zajda/Adobe Stock, 16–17; 9wooddy/Shutterstock, 17; MIXA next/Getty, 18–19, 23bl; Africa Studio/Shutterstock, 22 (jar); Ivonne Wierink/Shutterstock, 22; Dave Pot/Shutterstock, 24; figen tekin/Shutterstock, 24 (girl).

Printed in the United States of America at Corporate Graphics in North Mankato, Minnesota.

Table of Contents

Thank You

The sun is warm.

Flowers bloom.

We are grateful for sunny days.

To be grateful
is to be thankful.

Rae gets a gift.
She is grateful.
She writes a
thank you note.

Dear Nanna,

Thank you for

my Present. 🙂

X X X X

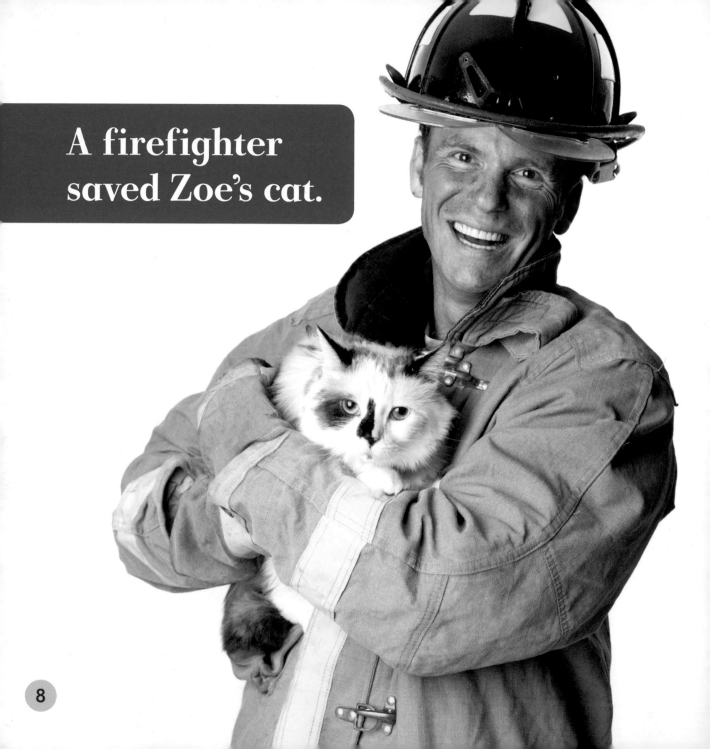

A firefighter saved Zoe's cat.

She bakes him cookies.

This is how she says thank you.

9

Ms. Sun is our teacher.

She teaches us something new every day.

We thank her.

Lee is grateful for his wheelchair.

It helps him go fast!

We play outside.

muscles

We are grateful for our muscles.

They make us strong.

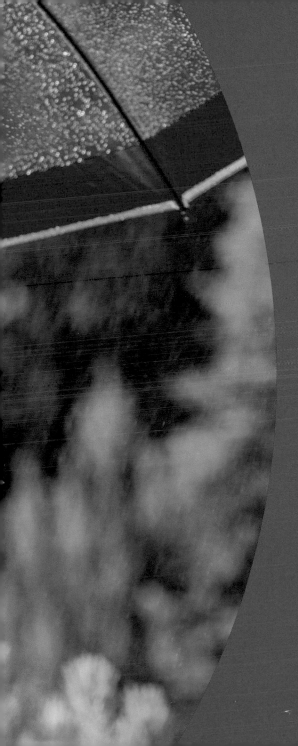

Oh, no! It is raining!

But Deb is grateful.

Why?

Rain helps plants grow.

It is time to eat.

We say grace.

We give thanks
for our food.

18

What are you grateful for?

Thank You Jar

Practice being grateful by making a Thank You Jar.

You will need:
- an empty glass jar
- safety scissors
- construction paper
- a pencil

Directions:
❶ Cut paper into square notes.
❷ Each day, write something you are grateful for on one of the notes. Is it something you have? Is it something you did? Is it a person?
❸ Fold the note. Put it in the jar.
❹ At the end of the week, read your notes.
❺ Keep adding more. It feels good to be grateful!

Picture Glossary

bloom
To grow
and open.

muscles
Body parts that
give you the
power to push,
pull, and lift.

grace
A short prayer
before a meal.

wheelchair
A chair with
wheels that
people who
cannot walk use
to get around.

Index

To Learn More

Learning more is as easy as 1, 2, 3.

1) Go to www.factsurfer.com

2) Enter "beinggrateful" into the search box.

3) Click the "Surf" button to see a list of websites.

With factsurfer.com, finding more information is just a click away.